BAKING COOKBOOK FOR YOUNG CHEF

The Friendly Cookbook with tips and tricks to Inspire Young Bakers. Delicious and Funny Recipes to Make with your Kids

By

Michael Donovan

Table of Contents

Introduction

If you're learning to bake, you will find that working with the dough and mashing it is surely a great way to release some stress from a long school day or long week. You might have some knowledge about cooking kitchen how-to, probably you´ve baked cookies before with your family or friends. Or probably you know nothing at all about cooking and that's alright as well because with this book you will learn how to become a pro in cooking.

When we think of baking, most of us conjure up images of cookies, breads, cakes, pies—well, desserts! That's definitely part of it, but other baking options that we'll explore include appetizers, pizzas, and quiche, to name a few. At its core, baking is the act of cooking something, usually flour-based foods, with dry heat (like in an oven). Baking is a little different than cooking, and sometimes trickier! With many baking recipes, there is a science behind the recipe.

The following chapters will discuss everything you need to know about cooking so you can make delicious meals for your friends and family. These recipes are sure to impress and satisfy anyone who comes to your table. In these chapters, you will find all the information you will need to go from a beginner's understanding of baking and how it works to an intermediate level that will allow you to prepare a large meal for everyone you love to enjoy! Whether you're looking to learn how to bake muffins for a friend or make a flatbread pizza, this book can help you to get the information you need. The information in this book will fill you with confidence and allow you to try all sorts of new and delicious things.

This book will help you learn lessons for baking success, as well as many baking tricks and tips along the way that might surprise your older family members, as well! Get ready to:

Explore your kitchen and learn what baking tools, appliances, bake ware, cookware, and pantry items can really help make you a baking pro.

Master baking skills such as how to measure ingredients, mix and fold, cream butter and sugar, create perfect dough, and melt chocolate, so you'll be ready to move onto more junior master chef baking recipes in no time.

Discover a world of sweet and savory baking recipes you can try, from basic to more junior master chef delicacies, as well as classics to new favorites. Let's get baking— you'll soon see it's "a piece of cake!"

Not only does this book include instructions on baking recipes but it also includes step-by-step details, equipment, preparation time, kitchen basics, and most importantly, tips on how to bake delicious recipes

Chapter 1:

The basics of baking

Your pantry is where the ingredients await! And the first rule of thumb for delicious baked goods: start with quality ingredients. It's important to have the right ingredients, but it's just as important that your ingredients are fresh and of the best quality. In some cases, you can substitute ingredients when you don't have the right thing, but sometimes substituting ingredients in baked goods can have disappointing results. Here are some common ingredients used in many baking recipes.

Baking Powder

This powder is a leavening agent—it makes baked goods rise. Store this in a dry, dark, cool place. You can check the expiration date, but it should usually be replaced every six to twelve months. Here's a fun experiment to test if baking powder is still good: Stir about 1 teaspoon baking powder into ⅓ cup hot water. If the mixture produces a lot of bubbles, the baking powder is still good to use.

Butter

Butter is used in many baking recipes. There are two main types of butter, unsalted and salted. Most baking recipes will call for unsalted butter, so you can control the amount of salt by adding it separately. Check your recipe to see if the butter should be cold, softened to room temperature, or melted. Don't substitute one for another, even if you're in a hurry. Also, don't substitute margarine or oil for butter unless the recipe says it's okay. Butter can be kept at room temperature for a short amount of time, but generally should be kept refrigerated.

Chocolate

This wildly popular delicacy comes in many types: unsweetened, dark, bittersweet, and semisweet are some of the most common. Unsweetened chocolate (which doesn't taste so great by itself) usually comes in bar form, while dark, bittersweet, and semisweet can be found as chips or bars. Unsweetened cocoa powder is called for in some baking recipes. This is a powder and contains no sugar. Chocolate lasts for a long time, but for best results, it should be stored in a dry, dark, cool place. Storing chocolate in the fridge is not recommended because the chocolate may "bloom," forming a gray film on the outside caused by the cocoa butter separating from the chocolate. It's safe to eat, but not so pretty to look at!

Cream and Milk

Whipped cream, made from cream, is a yummy and festive addition over many baked goods. If you're not familiar with cream, look out for the different types of cream next time you're in the grocery store. Heavy cream is the richest type of liquid cream, made up of at least 36 percent fat. Whipping cream has a fat content between 30 and 36 percent. Heavy cream and whipping cream should both be stored in the refrigerator. Either can be used in most cases but whipping heavy cream will result in a more stable, slightly thicker whipped cream.

Milk also comes in different fat contents. Whole milk is the highest in fat, followed by 2 percent, 1 percent, and then skim (fat-free). When baking with milk, a higher fat content milk will result in a moister and finer-textured baked good.

With both cream and milk, check the expiration date on the container before using; a sniff test will also tell you if your dairy is past its freshness. In general, both cream and milk should be used within two weeks of opening.

Baking techniques and skills

Baking isn't very different from making crafts. You need instructions (called a "recipe"), the right tools (measuring cups and mixing bowls, for example), and a little time. The bonus? You end up with something delicious to eat when you are done. Here are a few things you need to know before you start.

When it comes to cooking, the more organized you are, typically the more successful you will be. Check out these tips to prep and cook like a pro.

Reading a Recipe

It is so exciting to take a pile of ingredients and transform them into a finished dish! However, understanding a recipe before you begin is the most important step.

Read the whole recipe, two or three times. Relax, sit down, and

really

 read the recipe through. Pay attention to the order of the recipe. It's usually written that way for a reason.

Recipes are broken down into components. Reading, understanding, preparing for, and following the various parts of a recipe are what set you up for success. Here are all the parts of a recipe:

Baking techniques

Once you are done with the important skills in baking, you should explore these baking techniques that will take your career to the next level.

Preheating oven

I know you may be asking yourself, why preheat the oven? Because ovens need to be hot before you start baking. Simply turn on the oven to the stated temperature as you make preparations. The interesting thing to note is, electric ovens are efficient compared to gas ovens. This isn't a call for alarm; otherwise, you should be patient and ready to adjust your oven temperature accordingly.

Preparing baking pan or tin

There is nothing intimidating like a falling off cake when trying to get it out of the baking dish. To avoid disappointments from your precious treat, line the pan with parchment paper or generously grease the base and sides of the pan with butter. For spring form pans, however, lining the pan isn't vital since you will obviously remove the sides. But it will help the cake look more rustic. Finally, sometimes the sides will stick which is normal so no need to panic. Use a small knife to separate the cake from the tin being careful not to cut the cake.

Measuring ingredients

Baking is more scientific than the general cooking and that is why the ratio of ingredients should be strictly measured as stated on the recipe. That being said, the easiest, quickest and most accurate way of measurement is the use of a digital scale. If you don't have access to a scale, stick to cups and spoon but be ready for conversions. Not easy but the end results are worth it.

Rubbing in

The secret behind a light, crisp pastry to make short crust pastry, scones or scrambles is to get the butter coat as much flour as possible. You don't want melted butter in the pastry so use cool butter. Use fingertips to pick up the little butter pinches or pulse with the food processor until the mixture is as coarse as breadcrumbs.

Creaming method

Just like whisking eggs, creaming is a way of incorporating air in the baking goods making the mixture fluffier and lighter. What's important is not to use butter directly from the fridge. Allow it to soften at room temperature before using your hand mixer to mix. You can also use a food processor, but the hand mixture does an excellent job.

Whisking eggs

Just like the creaming method, this is a way of getting air into your creation making it fluffier and lighter. The best and easy way to do this is by use of a hand mixer which is less labor-intensive compared to the old-fashioned way which is therapeutic. Although this sounds easy, you should watch for over mixing. It has never happened to me, to be honest, but I think in that case they start to separate again which is bad.

Folding

This is the act of combining the light mixture or ingredient with the heavy ones preserving as much air as possible. This is easily done by carefully cutting through the mixture using a spoon edge and gently working with a figure of eight. The bowl should also move as you mix. You should also not forget to scrape the base and sides to ensure everything is well combined.

Kneading dough

Kneading dough refers to working on or stretching the dough by use of electric dough hook or hands. The process evenly incorporates all the ingredients and air in the dough. Additionally, the dough gets softer, smoother and develops gluten elasticity in the flour.

Rolling out

Rolling out may not sound complex but this is a tricky stage in the pastry. You need to be as cool as possible while you roll out your pastry on a floured surface. Moreover, you should use short and even strokes ensuring that you don't turn the pastry over but spin it through a quarter turn.

Shaping and cutting

After a successful rolling out of the pastry, it can be shaped and cut into the desired shapes. This can be done by the use of pastry cutters to cut shapes, biscuits and scones, or hands to shape bread rolls.

Piping

Piping is all about attaining pretty and even shapes. All you need is to spoon the mixture in a zip lock bag, press the cake mixture to one corner, twist the top then use a pair of scissors to cut off the corner. You are good to go! Patiently pipe your desired shapes. Most importantly, the size of the corner snip makes all the difference; large, the mixture will rush. too small, the mixture will take ages to flow out. Find the right size plus you can always transfer the mixture to a new zip lock bag.

Baking

Finally, we are here! Your oven should be preheated unless the recipes state otherwise. We said baking is an art, so you need to be careful and creative. If your cake starts to brown quickly before the center is cooked, cover the baking dish with a foil to retard browning. The most important point to note is that every time you open the oven door, you lose heat lengthening your baking time.

How to know baking is done

First and foremost, look at the color. If not golden brown enough to your liking, keep baking. Secondly, have a feel. I know you want your cakes slightly form and spongy. Be careful the cake is hot. For brownies, I consider mine ready once they have a crust even though they are a little under baked. Of course, you want that awesome squidgy texture. Thirdly, if you are not sure if the cake is ready, stab it with a knife or skewer. If it comes out clean then you good to go otherwise, bake a little longer.

Cooling

Note that even after removing the cake from the oven, it's still cooking. You can either cool the cake in the baking pan on a wire rack or remove the cake from the pan and cool it on a cake rack. If your cake is over baked, it's wise to remove it from the baking dish since you want it to cool quickly otherwise, cooling in the tin is the best.

Storing

Trust me sometimes it's not advisable to eat everything in a single sitting. I know it's hard fighting those sweet cravings while you have a banana caramel cake in a fridge. You, however, need to spare some for tomorrow. Moreover, you need to know the dos and don'ts of preserving food in your fridge. For example, cover anything involving cream and butter, chocolate goes dull when stored in a fridge.

Chapter 2:

Nutritional values explained

Nutrition Facts

2.0g

Amount Per Serving

Calories 0

	% Daily Values*
Total fat 0g	0%
Sodium 0mg	0%
Total Carbohydrate 0g	0%
Sugars 0g	0%
Protein 0g	0%

* Percentage Daily Values are based on a 2000 calorie diet

Pack Contents: 25 natural unbleached teabags 25x2g

NET WT 50g

You want to make sure that your daily intake (how much you're eating) of each thing isn't too much and that you're getting all the right vitamins, fats, minerals, calories, proteins, and more. These labels help you to know all about what's really in your food, and how much you should be eating. For instance, did you know that some of your favorite crunchy, cheesy snacks are only supposed to be eaten by about a handful at a time? These labels tell you all kinds of things about the foods you're eating.

The facts on these labels often cover:

- How many servings are in the whole container (box, bag, etc.) (A serving is how much of something you should be eating in one sitting)

- How big a serving size is in cups, ounces, grams, etc.

- How many calories are in each serving?

- How much of each nutrient such as protein and fat are in each serving?

- How many vitamins and minerals are in each serving?

- The percentage of your daily values that each of those numbers represents.

Daily values are how much of each nutrient you're supposed to get in each day. So, if this label says that 8g of fat is 10% of your daily value, you can do a little bit of math to find that the total daily recommended value of fat is ten times that, or 80g. By looking at these nutritional facts labels, we can know more about what's in the foods we're eating, and it can help us to make sure that our bodies are getting all the things they should be getting, while not getting too much of the things that we should only have in small amounts.

Sodium is one of the things that you will want to monitor as you get older. Eating too much sodium from day to day can cause some problems in your body and can cause your health to drop in ways that aren't too pleasant. You don't want to feel less than your best because you're not eating all the right things, right? These labels can help us to stay within the recommended daily limits of these things, so we stay nice and healthy. Thanks to these labels, we can know all the things that are in the foods we're eating, we can make sure that we're not having too many of the bad things, we can have more of the good things, and we can feel great while we're doing it.

One of the things you've probably heard people talking about watching their carbohydrate intake. Carbohydrates come from starchy or sugary foods like potatoes and fruit, as well as things like chips and candy. Some people like to limit their carbohydrates to about 200 grams each day, while people who are very active and who have careers in sports or fitness will tend to have lots more because they need the energy.

Calories is one of the things that people will tend to count the most, which is why it's one of the biggest numbers on the Nutritional Facts label. It's recommended that people who are trying to maintain their weight (which means that they're not trying to lose or gain weight) take in about 2,000 calories each day. Doing this gives you enough energy to get through your day without getting groggy and tired but doesn't give you so many calories that you start to put on weight. Your doctor can tell you just how many calories you should be eating each day in order to keep yourself feeling healthy and strong.

Preparing Your Table

When you're getting ready to bake, the first thing you want to do is make sure that your table, counter, or workspace is completely clear. You don't want to be moving things, washing dishes, and digging through the cabinets for the ingredients you need while you're in the middle of baking unless you have the downtime to do so.

Here's a little checklist that you can use to make sure that you've gotten all your tasks lined up in just the right way, so your baking process goes as smoothly as possible!

- Have all the dishes I will need been washed and dried already?

- Is the sink clear of dirty dishes, so I won't need to wash or move them while I'm trying to bake?

- Have all my tools been cleaned, dried, and laid out for me to use?

- Have all my ingredients been laid out so I can access them easily?

- Do I have all the seasonings and condiments that I will need in order to make my creation delicious?

- Have I set my oven to preheat at the right temperature?

Going down this checklist and making sure that you've gotten everything you need is a great way to save yourself a lot of time in the kitchen. There are few things worse than being at a critical stage when you need to add an ingredient, only to find that you don't have it laid out in front of you. This means that you need to run and find the ingredient and hope that nothing got messed up when you were looking. In many cases, when you're baking, your hands will be covered with butter, flour, oil, or some other mess and you will need to pay your way through the cabinets with greasy fingers or wash your hands and start all over again on your mixing once you've got the ingredients that you need.

Making sure that you have everything you need doesn't need to look like it does on cooking shows. You don't need a hundred little bowls with all your ingredients in them laid out before you, and you don't need to use every dish in the house just to bake. If this works for you and you prefer to do things this way, that is perfectly fine.

One piece of advice that can help you if you're choosing to run your kitchen in this way is to wash dishes as you go. You will reach certain stages in the baking process when your dough needs to rest or when your creation is in the oven. When you're waiting for things like this, go ahead and rinse or wash your dishes and clean your sink out. You will find that if you decide not to do this, your kitchen will look like a whole bag of flour exploded in the middle of it and took every dish in the kitchen along with it. Taking five minutes while your creations are rising or baking can make a world of difference at the end of your labors when your creation is golden brown and delicious, and the kitchen is spotless in spite of all that went on in there.

Preparation is key when you're working in the kitchen, but so is leaving the kitchen the way you found it. If you don't own the home, you're baking in; it can make your parents or the people who live in your home feel like they're being crowded with lots of dirty dishes. If you wash as you go, you won't feel like the dishes take very long at all!

Kid chef tips

Never be caught without butter again. Butter freezes great, so pop a pound in the freezer for those uh-oh moments.

Recipe Title

The recipe title is a good indicator of what to expect from a recipe.

Recipe Yield:

The yield or number of servings in a recipe helps you understand how many people it will feed and is a great indicator of whether you should double or even halve the recipe to meet your needs.

Ingredients:

The list of ingredients and their corresponding amounts and measurements set the tone for how the recipe will flow. Typically, ingredients are listed in the order of their use. Setting out your ingredients prior to beginning a recipe is a pro tip. Once you think you are finished prepping a recipe, read the ingredient list again make sure you remembered all the ingredients.

Instructions/Directions:

The instructions or directions of a recipe are the steps you need to take to create a chosen recipe.

Equipment/Tools Needed:

The equipment/tools needed section is there for you to

set out most of what you'll need to cook or bake a recipe.
Temperature and Time:
Typically in the first step of a recipe, it tells you if you need to preheat your oven and if so to what temperature. Additionally, stove-top recipes will tell you in various steps how high to set the stove and how long to cook or bake a recipe. Sometimes the time stated is a guide due to oven temperatures and proteins (meats/poultry/seafood) varying in size and weight.

Chapter 3:

Cakes, cupcakes, and cakes in a jar

Beginner

Chocolate Cake in a Jar

Preparation Time: *30 minutes*

Cooking Time: 40 minutes

Servings: 2

Ingredients:

1 cup al purpose flour

1 cup white sugar

1/2 tablespoon baking soda

1/4 tablespoon cinnamon, ground

1/3 cup butter

1/4 cup water

3 tablespoon cocoa powder, unsweetened

1/4 cup buttermilk

1 egg, beaten

1/2 tablespoon vanilla extract

1/4 walnuts, chopped

Direction:

Preheat oven to 325 degrees F. Wash the canning jars then dry them.

Mix flour, sugar, baking soda and ground cinnamon in a mixing bowl.

Add butter, water and cocoa powder in a saucepan and heat until all the butter has melted.

Transfer to a bowl.

Stir in the dry ingredients and blend well. Add milk, eggs, and vanilla and continue to mix until smooth.

Stir in the walnuts then divide the cake mix between the 2 jars.

Place the jars on a cooking sheet and bake for 40 minutes.

Let the cake cool then serve and enjoy.

Nutrition: calories 1024, fat 12, fiber 6, carbs 15, protein 5

Intermediate

Caramel Nut Cake in a Jar

Preparation Time: 30 minutes

Cooking Time: 40 minutes

Servings: 6

Ingredients:

3-1/2 cups all-purpose flour

1 tablespoon baking powder

2 tablespoon baking soda

1 tablespoon salt

2 cups brown sugar

2/3 cup white sugar

1 cup butter, softened

4 eggs

2/3 cup milk

1 tablespoon vanilla extract

1 cup walnuts, chopped

Direction:

Preheat oven to 325 degrees F. Wash the canning jars, dry them and grease them.

Sieve baking powder, flour, baking soda and salt in a medium mixing bowl.

In another bowl, mix white sugar, brown sugar, and butter until creamy.

Mix in eggs, milk, and vanilla until well combined.

Add dry mixture in wet mixture then mix until well combined. Fold in walnuts.

Divide the mixture among the 6 canning jars and wipe any batter on the rim.

Place the jars on a baking sheet and bake for 50 minutes.

Let cool before serving. Enjoy.

Nutrition: calories 1027, fat 42, fiber 4, carbs 15, protein 16

Chocolate Cake

Preparation time: 10 minutes

Cooking time: 20 minutes

Servings: 12

Ingredients:

2 cups of white sugar

A cup and a 3/4 of flour that is all-purpose

2 eggs

A single cup of milk

Half a cup of vegetable oil

¾ of a cup of cocoa powder that has been unsweetened

A single teaspoon and a half of baking powder

A single teaspoon and a half of baking soda

2 teaspoons of vanilla extract

A single cup of water that is boiling

Directions:

Heat the oven to 350 F.

Grease and flour 2 round pans that are 9 inches.

Get a bowl.

Mix everything in a bowl but the eggs, vanilla, and oil. Don't use the water yet either.

Stir everything together.

Add the oil, vanilla, and eggs, and the milk and mix for 2 minutes with a mixer on medium speed.

Stir in the water.

Pour in the pans.

Bake for a half-hour.

Cool for 10 minutes before you move to a wire rack.

Nutrition: calories 131, fat 7, fiber 7, carbs 12, protein 2

Junior master chef

Cheesecake

Preparation time: 10 minutes

Cooking time: 20 minutes

Servings: 12

Ingredients:

A single cup of sour cream

2 Teaspoons of vanilla

3 eggs

3 (8 ounce) packages of softened cream cheese

A third of a cup of divided sugar

A third of a cup of melted butter

A cup and ¾ of graham cracker crumbs

A single can of cherry pie filling (go for 21 ounces)

Directions:

Heat your oven to 350.

Mix the crumbs, sugar and butter and press into a spring form pan that is 9 inches.

Beat the cream cheese and leftover sugar using a mixer.

Mix until it is blended.

Go one at a time and beat it all on low speed.

Pour it over the crust.

Bake for 60 minutes.

You can top it with the filling.

Nutrition: calories 342 fat 7, fiber 7, carbs32, protein 7

Easy Chocolate Cupcakes

Preparation time: 15minutes

Cooking time: 20 minutes

Servings: 10

Ingredients

300g dark chocolate, break into chunks

200g self-rising flour

200g light muscovado sugar

6 tbsp cocoa

150ml sunflower oil

284ml pot soured cream

2 eggs

1 tbsp vanilla extract

3 tbsp light muscovado sugar for icing

Direction

Preheat the oven to 350°F . Line the cupcake tins with papers case then set-aside.

Whizz 100g of chocolate chips into small pieces in your food processor.

Add flour, sugar, cocoa, sunflower oil, 100ml cream, eggs, vanilla and 100ml water in a mixing bowl. Use a hand mixer to mix until smooth and well combined.

Stir in the whizzed chocolate chips then divides the mixture among the cases.

Bake for 20 minutes then place on a cooling rack.

To make the icing, mix the remaining chocolate chips, cream, 3 tbsp sugar in a saucepan.

Gently heat until the chocolate chips melts. Chill the icing in a fridge then swirl it on the cupcake.

Serve and enjoy.

Nutrition: calories 544, fat 31, fiber 0, carbs 15, protein 6

Chapter 4:

Pies, tarts and pastries

Beginner

Mixed fruit tart

Preparation time: 25minutes

Cooking time: 35 minutes

Servings: 8

Ingredients

220g plain flour plus a handful for dusting

1 tbsp golden caster sugar

110g butter, unsalted, chilled and diced

1 large egg yolk

120g mascarpone

250ml double cream

1 tbsp vanilla bean paste

1 tbsp icing sugar

300g fruit (cherries, redcurrants, and berries)

Direction

Preheat your oven to 350OF.

Pulse flour, sugar, and salt in a food processor to make the pastry. Add butter and continue to pulse until a coarse consistency is achieved.

Add egg yolk and 3 tablespoons of water then pulse the mixture starts to come together.

Use your hands to bring the dough together on a work surface. Wrap it in a cling film and let it rest for an hour.

Roll out the pastry on a floured surface to line a 23cm tart tin. Trim any excess hanging on the edges then let rest for 30 minutes.

Use a fork to prick the pastry then line with a crumpled baking parchment paper. Fill with baking beans and bake for 20 minutes.

Remove the beans and parchment paper then bake the pastry for 12 more minutes.

Take the pastry out of the tin and let it rest to cool completely.

Make the filling by mixing mascarpone, double cream, vanilla, and icing sugar until creamy.

Spread the cream on the pastry in an even layer. Decorate with fruits of your choice.

Serve and enjoy when fresh.

Nutrition: calories 454, fat 32, fiber 2, carbs 31, protein 5

Plum Pie with Custard

Preparation time: 10 minutes

Cooking time: 50 minutes

Servings: 8

Ingredients:

2 pounds ripe plums (stoned and cut into thick slices)

5 ounces golden caster sugar

⅛ tbsp ground cloves

1 heaped tbsp cornflour

Flour (to dust)

1 (17 ounces) pack shortcrust pastry

1 egg (beaten, to glaze)

Pinch granulated sugar

Custard:

4 egg yolks

3 ounces caster sugar

1 cup milk

1 cup double cream

1 vanilla pod (seeds scraped)

Directions:

Preheat the main oven along with a large baking sheet to 390 degrees F.

Add the plums, caster sugar, and cloves in a pan and simmer for 8-10 minutes, until the sugar is dissolved and the plums, juicy.

In a small bowl, combine the corn flour with a drop of the plum juices and mix thoroughly into the fruit. Boil for 2-3 minutes, stirring, until it thickens.

To prepare the custard: In a bowl, blend the egg yolks with the sugar.

Next, in a pan, heat the milk with the double cream and vanilla pod scrapings until almost boiling, and pour slowly onto the egg mix, whisking continually.

Return to a clean pan and gently heat while stirring until the mixture thickens and easily coats the back of a spoon. Allow to cool quickly, and transfer to the fridge to chill.

On a clean, lightly floured surface, roll ⅔ of the pastry out.

Use the pastry to line a pie dish, allowing the pastry to hang over the pan's edges.

Fill the pastry with the plums.

Roll the remaining ⅓ of pastry so that it is approximately 1" larger than the pie dish and drape it over the plums. Pinch the edges together, make a small hole in the top of the pie, to allow the steam to escape.

Next, brush the top of the pie with beaten egg and scatter over the sugar.

Place the pie on the preheated baking sheet and bake in the oven until golden, for 25-30 minutes.

Serve the pie, hot, with the custard.

Nutrition: calories 456 fat 7, fiber 5 carbs 5, protein 8

Intermediate

Mince Pies

Preparation time: 10 minutes

Cooking time: 50 minutes

Servings: 16

Ingredients:

Pastry:

13 ounces plain flour

9 ounces unsalted butter (softened)

4½ ounces caster sugar

1 large egg (beaten)

1 beaten egg (to glaze)

Mince Pies:

1 (21 ounces) large jar mincemeat

2 Satsumas (segmented)

1 eating apple (cored and diced small)

Zest 1 lemon

Icing sugar (to dust)

Directions:

Add the flour and butter to a bowl, and rub to a crumb-like consistency.

Next, add the sugar and 1 beaten egg and mix well to combine.

Tip the mixture out onto a lightly-floured clean work surface and fold until the pastry starts to come together while taking care not to over-mix.

Wrap the pastry in kitchen wrap and transfer to the fridge to chill for 10 minutes.

Spoon the mincemeat into a bowl. Then, add the Satsuma segments, followed by the chopped apple and lemon zest.

Next, preheat the main oven to 425 degrees F.

Roll the pastry out to a 1" thickness.

Using a 4" circular pastry cutter, cut out 16 circles of pastry and place them in a muffin tray.

Spoon 1½ tablespoons of the mincemeat mixture into each pastry circle. Brush the edge of each pie with beaten egg.

Re-roll the pastry out, and cut out 16 (2¾") circles for the pie lids. Lay the pie lids on top of the filling to cover, and seal. Glaze the pastry with beaten egg, and scatter over a sprinkling of caster sugar. Finally, make a couple of small cuts in the top of the pastry tops.

Then, bake the pies in the preheated oven until golden brown, for 15-20 minutes. Allow the pies to cool before removing them from the muffin trays.

Lastly, dust with a sprinkling of icing sugar and serve.

Nutrition: calories 176, fat 7, fiber 7, carbs 12, protein 10

Junior master chef

Peanut Butter Cup Pie

Preparation Time: *15 minutes*

Cooking Time: 20 minutes

Servings: 12

Ingredients:

8 ounces milk chocolate, chopped

1 cup heavy cream

1 cup creamy peanut butter

2 cups thin pretzel sticks, smashed into pieces

1 (9-inch) ready-made chocolate piecrust

Directions:

Preparing the Ingredients. In 2-quart saucepan, combine chocolate and 1/2 cup cream.

Cook over low heat for 4 to 5 minutes or until chocolate melts, stirring. Pour half of chocolate into medium-size bowl; set aside.

Remove saucepan from heat. Stir in peanut butter until blended. Cool completely.

In another large container with mixer on medium-high speed, beat remaining 1/2 cup cream until stiff peaks form

Refrigerate. With rubber spatula, fold whipped cream and 1 cup pretzels into peanut-butter mixture until blended. Spread in piecrust.

Spread reserved chocolate mixture on top; cover evenly with remaining 1 cup pretzels. Refrigerate for 4 hours or until firm.

Nutrition: Calories: 297 Total Fat: 18g Protein: 16g Fiber: 4g

Quick cottage pie

Preparation time: 10 minutes

Cooking time: 30 minutes

Servings: 4

Ingredients

100g pack mushrooms, halved

1 tbsp olive oil

1 tbsp plain flour

1/2 recipe multi minced

750g potatoes, quartered

75ml skimmed milk

2 springs onions, sliced thinly

Direction

Preheat the oven to 425OF.

Cook the mushrooms in oil in a non-stick skillet until browned.

Mix in plain flour and multi mince then cook until cooked through and the sauce is thickened.

Tip the mixture in an oven-safe dish.

Meanwhile, cook potatoes in a pot of salted water until soft. Drain and mash them together with skimmed milk.

Stir in half the onions then spoon the mixture in the dish.

Cook in the oven for 15 minutes or until the top is browned.

Sprinkle onions for garnish and enjoy.

Nutrition: calories 224, fat 12, fiber 5, carbs 15, protein 5

Chapter 5:

Cookies recipes

Beginner

Chocolate Peanut Butter Sandwich Cookies

Preparation time: 10 minutes

Cooking time: 20 minutes

Servings: 12

Ingredients

4 tablespoons yellow cake mix

2 tablespoon egg (beaten) or applesauce

½ tablespoon brown sugar

2 tablespoons peanut butter

1 teaspoon water

½ tablespoon oil

Topping:

Sugar

Chocolate frosting

Directions:

Preheat oven. Spray pans with nonstick spray

Mix cookie ingredients together in small bowl

Roll cookie mixture into 1 inch balls

Roll cookies in granulated sugar to coat

Place on pan and flatten into cookie shape

Place pan into the oven and cook for approximately 8-10 minutes

Remove cookies from oven and cool

Spread chocolate frosting of choice on bottom of two cookies and press together to form the chocolate peanut butter sandwich

Nutrition: calories 224, fat 12, fiber 5, carbs 15, protein 5

Edible Hands

Preparation time: 10 minutes

Cooking time: 20 minutes

Servings: 12

Ingredients

Refrigerated sugar cookie dough

All-purpose flour (optional)

Your choice of frosting and candies/ sprinkles to decorate

Directions:

Remove desired amount of dough from the wrapper

Grease Pans

Flatten cookie dough and cover the entire bottom of pan with it.

Place hand on top of cookie dough and press down to make a handprint

Carefully trim away excess dough from around handprint using a knife (Adult assistance required for this one)

Place pan and cookie into freezer for 15 minutes

Preheat Oven

Remove handprint from freezer and place in oven

Cook approximately 6-9 minutes until edges are golden brown

Cool Completely

Decorate hand using frosting and candies. Get creative here. You can use different candies for form a bracelet or a ring. You can also make "fingernails" on your hand by placing the same colored candy on the tip of each finger

Nutrition: calories 778, fat 42, fiber 1, carbs 15, protein 9

Intermediate

Fruity Fingers

Preparation time: 10 minutes

Cooking time: 20 minutes

Servings: 12

Ingredients (cookies):

Refrigerated sugar cookie dough

½ cup crushed Fruit flavored cereal (divided)

Directions:

Remove desired amount of cookie dough from wrapper (depending on how many cookies you want to make). Refrigerate remaining dough

Mix together 1 teaspoon crushed cereal and cookie dough

Roll dough into balls and refrigerate for 1 hour

Preheat oven and spray pans with nonstick spray

Roll cookie balls into 2-3 inch long "fingers" (ropes)

Coat cookies by rolling in cereal

Place cookies on sheet making sure to leave enough room between them (1-2 inches)

Bake until just slightly brown (usually 8-10 minutes)

Remove and allow cookies to cool completely

Tip: I used the spatula to gently "shape" cookies while still warm

Nutrition: calories 224, fat 12, fiber 5, carbs 15, protein 5

Strawberry Cups (from refrigerated cookie dough)

Preparation time: 10 minutes

Cooking time: 20 minutes

Servings: 12

Ingredients (cookies):

Refrigerated sugar cookie dough

All purpose flour (optional)

2 tablespoons strawberry preserves (*can choose a different flavor preserves if you prefer)

Directions:

Remove about 2-3 ounces of dough from the wrapper

Roll dough into ¾ inch balls

Using your thumb, press down in the center of each ball to form a deep indention making it look like a small "mini" bowl. Flatten slightly to fit in pan

Place cookies in freezer for 20 minutes

Preheat oven and spray pans with nonstick spray

Bake until edges are just slightly brown (usually 8-10 minutes

Remove from oven and press back down in center of cookie with the tip of a spoon to form your "mini" bowl again.

Place cookies back in oven and cook for an additional 2-3 minutes. Cookies should be golden brown

Remove from oven and cool cookies completely

Fill the center of your cookie with strawberry preserves

Nutrition: calories 224, fat 12, fiber 5, carbs 15, protein 5

Junior master chef

Basic Sandwich Cookies

Preparation time: 10 minutes

Cooking time: 20 minutes

Servings: 12

Ingredients (cookies):

Any flavor refrigerated cookie dough

All purpose flour (optional)

Filling:

Your choice of assorted frostings, ice cream or peanut butter

Sprinkles or assorted candies (ex. M&M's ™)

Directions:

Preheat oven. Spray pans with nonstick spray

Remove desired amount of cookie dough from wrapper (depending on how many cookies you want to make). Refrigerate remaining dough

Roll dough to ¼ inch thickness. You can sprinkle a little flour down first to keep the cookies from sticking if you'd like.

Cut out cookies using a small round cookie cutter

Place cookies on sheet making sure to leave enough room between them (1-2 inches)

Bake until edges are just slightly brown (usually 8-10 minutes)

Remove and allow cookies to cool completely

Spread desired filling on the underside of the 1st cookie. Top with the second cookie and press together

Roll cookie edges in sprinkles or assorted candies

Nutrition: calories 332, fat 12, fiber 1 carbs 35, protein 8

Chocolate Peanut Butter Cups (cookie dough)

Preparation time: 10 minutes

Cooking time: 20 minutes

Servings: 12

Ingredients (cookies):

Refrigerated chocolate cookie dough

All purpose flour (optional)

2 tablespoons peanut butter frosting (recipe in frosting section)

Directions:

Remove about 2-3 ounces of dough from the wrapper

Roll dough into ¾ inch balls

Using your thumb, press down in the center of each ball to form a deep indention making it look like a small "mini" bowl

Place cookies in freezer for 20 minutes

Preheat oven and spray pans with nonstick spray

Bake until edges are just slightly browned (usually 8-10 minutes

Remove from oven and press back down in center of cookie with the tip of a spoon to form your "mini" bowl again.

Place cookies back in oven and cook for an additional 2-3 minutes. Cookies should be firm and set

Remove from oven and cool cookies completely

Fill center of your cookie "bowl" with peanut butter frosting

Chapter 6:

Glazing and frostings recipes

Beginners

Vanilla Buttercream Frosting

Preparation time: 10 minutes

Cooking time: 20 minutes

Servings: 12

Ingredients:

4 tablespoons powdered sugar

1 tablespoon butter (softened)

¾ teaspoon milk

¼ teaspoon vanilla extract

Food coloring of choice (optional)

Directions:

Cream butter until smooth (can use a wooden spoon if needed)

Gradually add in powdered sugar and beat together until fluffy

Add in vanilla and milk

Beat until light and fluffy (3-5 minutes)

Add drop of food coloring of choice to frosting

Mix well

Nutrition: calories 444, fat 12, fiber 1, carbs 35, protein 8

Hot Chocolate Whipped Cream

Preparation time: 10 minutes

Cooking time: 20 minutes

Servings: 12

Ingredients:

½ cup heavy whipping cream

¼ cup hot chocolate mix

Directions:

Get whisk and bowl very cold by placing in freezer for about 15-20 minutes

Beat heavy whipping cream for about 2 minutes

Add hot chocolate mix to whipped cream

Continue to beat until it thickens and forms a stiff peak

Nutrition: calories 321, fat 14, fiber 5, carbs 25, protein 7

Cream Cheese Frosting

Preparation time: 10 minutes

Cooking time: 20 minutes

Servings: 12

Ingredients:

1 tablespoon unsalted butter (softened)

1 ounce cream cheese (softened)

1/8 teaspoon vanilla extract

Pinch salt

8 tablespoons powdered sugar

Directions:

Cream together butter and cream cheese until smooth

Add in salt and vanilla extract

Slowly add in powdered sugar until mixed well

Nutrition: calories 321, fat 55, fiber 1, carbs 7, protein 21

Chocolate Glaze

Preparation time: 10 minutes

Cooking time: 20 minutes

Servings: 12

Ingredients:

3 tablespoons powdered sugar

3/4 teaspoon milk

1/4 teaspoon vanilla extract

½ tablespoon cocoa powder

1/8 teaspoon butter (melted)

Directions:

Combine all ingredients and mix until creamy

Nutrition: calories 224, fat 12, fiber 5, carbs 15, protein 5

Vanilla Glaze

Preparation time: 10 minutes

Cooking time: 20 minutes

Servings: 12

Ingredients:

3 tablespoons powdered sugar

¾ teaspoon milk

Pinch salt

1/16 teaspoon vanilla extract

1/8 teaspoon butter (melted)

Directions:

Combine all ingredients and mix until creamy

Nutrition: calories 224, fat 12, fiber 5, carbs 15, protein 5

Lemonade Frosting

Preparation time: 10 minutes

Cooking time: 20 minutes

Servings: 12

Ingredients:

½ tablespoon presweetened lemonade flavor drink mix

1 teaspoon water

1 tablespoon butter (softened)

¾ teaspoon heavy whipping cream

4 tablespoons powdered sugar

Small drop yellow food color

Directions:

Mix all ingredients together in a bowl. Beat until light and fluffy

Nutrition: calories 145, fat 23, fiber 6, carbs 15, protein 3

Strawberry Buttercream

Preparation time: 10 minutes

Cooking time: 20 minutes

Servings: 12

Ingredients:

1 ½ tablespoons butter (softened)

6 tablespoons powdered sugar

1 heaping teaspoon strawberry puree (2 strawberries pureed in a mini food processor

¼ teaspoon strawberry jam

1/16 teaspoon vanilla extract (just a couple of drops)

Directions:

Cream butter until creamy and smooth

Slowly add in powdered sugar until mixed well

Add in the strawberry puree, the strawberry jam and the vanilla extract. Mix well

Can add additional powdered sugar or strawberry puree if needed (to thin or thicken up the frosting).

Use a spatula or piping bag to frost your bakery items

Nutrition: calories 134, fat 12, fiber 5, carbs 15, protein 5

Drink Mix (Kool-Aid™) Frosting

Preparation time: 10 minutes

Cooking time: 20 minutes

Servings: 12

Ingredients:

4 tablespoons powdered sugar

1 tablespoon butter (softened)

½ tablespoon milk

¼ teaspoon Kool-Aid™ unsweetened drink mix

Food coloring of choice (optional)

Directions:

Cream butter until smooth (can use a wooden spoon if needed)

Gradually add in powdered sugar and beat together until fluffy

Add in Kool-Aid™ and milk

Nutrition: calories 224, fat 12, fiber 5, carbs 15, protein 5

Chapter 7:

Bars recipes and baked snack recipes

Beginner

Lemon Bars

Preparation time: 10 minutes

Cooking time: 55 minutes

Servings: 15

Ingredients

1 cup softened butter, unsalted

1 tbsp vanilla extract

2-3/4 cups sugar, granulated and divided

1 tbsp salt

2-1/2 cups all-purpose flour, divided

6 eggs

3 lemons zest

3/4 cup lemon juice

Powdered sugar

Direction

Preheat your oven to 350oF.

Prepare a baking pan, 9x13", by sparing with cooking spray, non-stick. Set aside.

For the crust

Place butter, vanilla, 1/2 cup sugar, and salt in a bowl, medium, then whisk to combine. Use a hand mixer, electric.

Add 2 cups of all-purpose flour while whisking to obtain soft dough. Place the dough on your baking pan.

Press the dough with clean hands, a heavy glass bottom or a tamper until an even layer.

Transfer the pan into the oven middle rack.

Bake for about 15-18 minutes until the edges are lightly golden. Remove pan from the oven.

For the filling

Place eggs, lemon zest, 2-1/4 cups sugar, and lemon juice in a mixing bowl, large, then vigorously whisk until combined and smooth. Sift in 1/2 cup flour and continue to whisk until fully incorporated.

Pour the filling over your crust and place the pan back to the oven.

Bake for about 30-35 minutes until set and a toothpick gets out clean once inserted in the bar center.

Remove from the oven and let cool at room temperature for about 20 minutes.

Place in a fridge for about 2 hours then slice.

Generously splash with sugar and serve.

Nutrition: calories 370, fat 14, fiber 2, carbs 55, protein 5

S'mores Seven Layer Bars

Preparation time: 10 minutes

Cooking time: 30 minutes

Servings: 20

Ingredients

3/4 cup melted butter

2-1/2 cups Graham cracker crumbs

1 can (14-oz) condensed milk, sweetened

2 cups mini marshmallows

1 cup Graham cracker broken pieces

1 cup chocolate chips, semi-sweet

2, 1.55-oz, chocolate bars, into pieces

Direction

Preheat your oven to 350oF.

Prepare a baking dish, 9x13", by sparing with cooking spray, non-stick.

Mix butter and Graham cracker crumbs in a bowl, small, and then press the mixture into the baking dish. Top with condensed milk.

Splash with 1 cup marshmallows, Graham cracker pieces, and chocolate chips on top.

Bake for about 15 minutes.

Remove from the oven, splash with marshmallow remainder, and return back to the oven.

Bake for another 10-15 minutes until edges become golden and marshmallows are browned.

Now transfer onto a cooling rack for about 15 minutes then top with chocolate bar pieces.

Slice and serve.

Enjoy!

Nutrition: calories 190, fat 12, fiber 5, carbs 15, protein 2

Intermediate

Cinnamon Raisin Swirl Bread

Preparation Time: *10 minutes*

Cooking Time: 10 minutes

Servings: 20

Ingredients:

2 tablespoon milk

1-1/2 cups water, warm

1 tablespoon salt

2 tablespoon shortening

3 tablespoon white sugar

2 tablespoon yeast, active dry

4 cups bread flour

1 cup raisins

2 tablespoon brown sugar

2 tablespoon softened butter

1 tablespoon cinnamon, ground

1 tablespoon melted butter

Direction:

Place milk, water, salt, shortening, sugar, yeast, and flour in the bread machine pan. Use manufacturer's recommendation then select cycle and press start.

Add rising just 5 minutes before the kneading cycle is over if your bread machine has fruit setting.

Once the kneading cycle is over, remove dough and place on a surface that is lightly floured.

Roll your dough into a rectangle then spread with brown sugar, butter, and cinnamon. Divide into two equal parts.

Lightly grease two bread pans, 9x5inch, then place loaves in. Allow to rise 1 hour until double in size.

Meanwhile, preheat your oven to 350oF.

Brush the loaves top with melted butter and place into the oven.

Bake for about 30-40 minutes until a brown crust and a hollow sound when tapped.

Enjoy.

Nutrition: calories 59, fat 2, fiber 0, carbs 15, protein 1

Baked Eggs and Spinach in Sweet Potato Boats

Preparation Time: *5 minutes*

Cooking Time: 1 hour 15 minutes

Servings: 4

Ingredients:

2 sweet potatoes, large

Pepper and salt

1 tablespoon butter

1 cup finely chopped baby spinach, packed

4 eggs

Direction:

Preheat an oven to 400oF.

Bake sweet potatoes for about 45-60 minutes in the oven.

Halve each sweet potato and scoop most of its flesh out leaving a small flesh rim round the potato skin.

Season each half with pepper and salt.

Add butter cubes to each potato half then top with spinach. Season again with pepper and salt.

Break an egg carefully into each half.

Bake the potato halves in your preheated oven for about 15 minutes until the eggs cook to your liking.

Lastly, season once more with pepper and salt.

Serve and enjoy.

Nutrition: Calories: 159 Total fat: 7g Protein: 7g Fiber: 3g Sodium: 216mg

Junior master chef

Savory Keto Breakfast Cookies

Preparation Time: *5 minutes*

Cooking Time: 20 minutes

Servings: 12

Ingredients:

3 eggs, large

1-1/2 cups almond flour

1 tablespoon baking powder

1 cup finely shredded cheddar cheese

Black pepper

1/2 tablespoon salt

Optional:

3 cooked bacon strips, crumbled

1 minced scallion

Direction:

Preheat your oven to 350oF. Line the baking sheet with parchment paper.

Place eggs, almond flour, baking powder, cheese, black pepper, and salt in a mixing bowl. Mix using a rubber spatula until stiff and combined.

Fold in bacon and scallions if using.

Divide the mixture into mounds and place on the lined baking sheet, about 12 in a batch, and then smooth the edges into circular shape with slightly dampened fingers.

Flatten the mound tops until cookies of ¾ inch thick.

On the oven middle rack, bake the cookies for about 14-16 minutes until the edges are lightly golden and firm.

When through, let it out from the oven and let cool for about 5 minutes.

Serve and enjoy!

Nutrition: calories 160, fat 14, fiber 5, carbs 15, protein 8

Cheesy Baked Eggs

Preparation Time: *5 minutes*

Cooking Time: 15 minutes

Servings: 1

Ingredients:

1 tablespoon softened butter

2 tablespoon milk, half and half or cream

2 large eggs

Pinch of black pepper

Pinch of salt

2 tablespoon cheddar cheese, shredded

1 tablespoon parmesan cheese, grated

Direction:

Preheat your oven to 400oF.

In the meantime, coat inside of an oven ramekin, 8-ounces, with butter.

Whisk milk and eggs in a bowl, small.

Stir in pepper, salt, and cheeses.

Pour the batter into the ramekin.

For about 15-18 minutes, bake until eggs are cooked through.

Enjoy!

Nutrition: calories 358, fat 28, fiber 1, carbs 15, protein 5

Chapter 8:

Muffins crackers and Bite-size treats

Beginners

Ciabatta Bread

Preparation time: 30 minutes

Cooking time: 25 minutes

Servings: 23

Ingredients

1-1/2 cup water

1-1/2 tbsp salt

1 tbsp white sugar

1 tbsp olive oil

3-1/4 cup bread flour

1-1/2 tbsp bread machine yeast

Direction

Preheat oven to 3500F.Line a baking sheet and dust with flour

Add all the ingredients except oil in a stand mixer. Mix on low speed until well combined.

Add oil and mix for 5 more minutes. Divide the mixture into two parts and form each into 3 x 14-inch ovals.

Spritz loaves with water then bake for 30 minutes or until golden brown.

Let cool then serve and enjoy.

Nutrition: calories 73, fat 1, fiber 5, carbs 14, protein 3

Intermediate

Chocolate Pecan Pie Squares

Preparation Time: *25 minutes*

Cooking Time: 40 minutes

Servings: 16

Ingredients:

For the crust

Butter, for greasing the pan

3/4 cup all-purpose flour

1/8 Teaspoon table salt

4 tablespoons unsalted butter, at room temperature

2 tablespoons brown sugar

For the filling

1 large egg

1 large egg yolk

1/3 cup corn syrup

1/3 Cup granulated sugar

1 tablespoon unsweetened cocoa powder

1 tablespoon unsalted butter, melted

1/2 teaspoon vanilla extract

1/8 Teaspoon table salt

3/4 cup chocolate chips

3/4 cup coarsely chopped pecans

Directions:

Preheat the oven to 350 degrees F. Lightly grease an 8-inch square baking pan.

Make the crust. In a medium bowl, add the flour, 1/8 teaspoon of salt, 4 tablespoons of room-temperature brown sugar, and butter.

Beat with mixer till blended and crumbly. Press the crust in an even layer over the bottom of the prepared pan.

For 10 to 15 minutes bake, or until golden brown around the edges.

Make the filling.

Meanwhile, in a large container, whisk the egg, egg yolk, corn syrup, granulated sugar, cocoa powder, 1 tablespoon of melted butter, vanilla, and 1/8 teaspoon of salt with an electric mixer on medium speed until well blended.

Add chocolate chips and pecans and mix with a spoon.

Bake the pie squares. Take out the crust from the oven, and pour the filling evenly over the top of the crust.

For 20 to 25 minutes, bake or until the middle appears set. Cool completely before cutting into bars.

Nutrition: Calories: 397 Total Fat: 18g Protein: 16gFiber: 4g

Apple-Custard Bake

Preparation Time: *15 minutes*

Cooking Time: 30 minutes

Servings: 4

Ingredients:

4 tablespoons butter, cubed, plus more for greasing the pan

5 tablespoons flour

4 tablespoons sugar

Zest of 2 Meyer lemons

2/3 Cup whole milk

4 eggs

3 apples, stripped, cored, and cut into 1/2-inch wedges

Confectioners' sugar, for dusting

Directions:

Grease the pan. Butter a cast-iron skillet. Preheat the oven to 400 degrees F.

Mix the ingredients. In a medium container, mix together the flour, sugar, lemon zest, and milk. Add the eggs and beat vigorously.

As you pour the mixture into the pan, don't stop whisking.

Arrange the fruit. Fan the apple wedges and lay them onto the mixture. It's okay if they slide a little as you arrange them.

Bake the custard. Dot the surface with butter, and bake until the custard puffs and has turned golden brown at the edges, about 30 minutes.

Serve. Dust confectioners' sugar onto the custard.

Nutrition: Calories: 297 Total Fat: 18g Protein: 16g Fiber: 4g

Junior master chef

Super Easy Banana Muffins

Preparation Time: *15 minutes*

Cooking Time: 25 minutes

Servings: 10

Ingredients:

2 large bananas

1/2 cup sugar, granulated

1/3 cup canola oil

1/2 tablespoon vanilla extract

1/4 cup sugar, light brown

1 eggs, large

1 tablespoon cinnamon

1-1/2 cups all-purpose flour

1/2 tablespoon baking soda

1/2 tablespoon salt

1 tablespoon baking powder

Direction:

Preheat your oven to 425oF.

In a 12-cavity muffin pan, line 10 cavities with cupcake liners.

Place mashed bananas, granulated sugar, canola oil, vanilla, brown sugar, and egg in a mixing bowl, large, then vigorously whisk until combined and smooth.

Add cinnamon, flour, baking soda, salt, and baking powder to the mixing bowl and continue whisking until combined. Be careful to over-mix.

Divide equally the mixture among the cupcake liners then place the muffin pan to your oven.

Bake for about 5 minutes at 425oF.

Now reduce temperature to 350oF and continue to bake for about 14-16 minutes until a toothpick comes out clean when inserted.

Remove the muffin pan and let cool for about 5 minutes.

Serve and enjoy!

Nutrition: calories 210, fat 12, fiber 3, carbs 15, protein 6

Chapter 9:

Savory breads and snacks

Beginners

Smoky Pretzel Mix

Preparation Time: 10 minutes

Cooking Time:40 minutes

Serving: 8

Ingredients:

A single cup of almonds that are smoked

A single cup of mini pretzels

2 teaspoons of chipotle chili powder

A single teaspoon of paprika that is smoked

2 cups corn snack crackers

2 cups of rice cereal squares

2 cups of white cheddar cheese crackers in bite-size

6 tablespoons of butter that is unsalted

Directions:

Heat the oven to 325.

Toss everything together except the butter and spices in a bowl.

Melt the butter in a pan over medium heat.

Stir in chili powder, paprika, and garlic.

Drizzle over the mix.

Toss to coat evenly.

Spread it on a rimmed baking sheet that you lined with parchment paper.

Bake for 12 minutes. Stir once during this time.

Cool totally on the sheet.

Store in a container that is airtight.

Nutrition: calories 570, fat, fiber 5, carbs 50, protein 12

Almond-Raisin Granola

Preparation Time: 30 minutes

Cooking Time: 1 hours

Serving: 2

Ingredients:

Half a cup of flax seeds

Half a cup of sunflower seed kernels

A cup of raw almonds that are sliced

3 cups of oats that are old-fashioned

A quarter cup of melted coconut oil

A single cup of raisins

6 tablespoons of honey

6 tablespoons of pure maple syrup

2 tablespoons of water that is warm

Directions:

Heat your oven to 250 and line a jelly roll pan with baking parchment.

Mix everything but the water, oil, honey, and syrup in a bowl and whisk the water, oil, honey, and syrup in another bowl. Make sure that the honey mix is smooth.

Pour the oat mix bowl into the honey bowl.

Spread the mix on the pan in a layer that is even.

Bake for an hour but up to an hour and a half until the color is a golden brown.

Take out of the oven and make sure that you let it cool completely.

Take the granola off by lifting the paper.

Break it and place in a bowl adding your choice of ingredients and then mix it.

Store in a container that is airtight.

Nutrition: calories 570, fat, fiber 5, carbs 50, protein 12

Intermediate

Blueberry Pound Cake

Preparation Time: 20minutes

Cooking Time: 1 hours 30 minutes

Serving: 8

Ingredients:

2 Tablespoons of butter

A quarter cup of white sugar

2 ¾ cups of all-purpose flour

A single teaspoon of baking powder

A single cup of butter

4 eggs

2 cups of white sugar

2 cups of blueberries that are fresh

A single teaspoon of vanilla extract

A quarter cup of flour that is all-purpose

Directions:

Preheat your oven to 325 F.

Grease a pan that is 10 inches with 2 tablespoons of butter.

Sprinkle that same pan with a quarter cup of sugar.

Mix 2 ¾ of the cup of flour with the baking powder and place it to the side.

Get a bowl and cream a cup of butter and 2 cups of sugar together until it has become fluffy and light.

Beat the eggs one at a time before stirring the vanilla in.

Slowly beat in your flour mix.

Dredge your berries with the last quarter cup of flour.

Fold into the batter before pouring it in your prepared pan.

Bake for 80 minutes. The toothpick test should show a clean toothpick.

Let cool for 10 minutes into the pan before letting it totally cool on a wire rack.

Nutrition: calories 340, fat 12, fiber 5, carbs 45, protein 6

Jam Pockets

Preparation Time: 10 minutes

Cooking Time: 2 hours

Serving: 8

Ingredients:

A single teaspoon of vanilla

A single egg

2 cups of flour

Half a cup of powdered sugar

A single cup of butter that is cut into cubes and cold

Directions:

Preheat your oven to 375.

Use a food processor and combine your sugar and flour until they have mixed.

Toss in your butter and give it a few long buzzes with it until it has a cornmeal look.

Add the vanilla and egg and then buzz it twice more. You should be left with a soft dough.

Cover with plastic wrap and then let it chill in the fridge for a couple of hours.

Roll out our dough and use a cookie cutter to make circles.

Add the jam of your choice to the center and fold your edges inward. It should overlap in the

middle.

Bake 10 minutes.

The bottom should be a faint brown color.

When cooled, sprinkle sugar over the top.

This recipe will give you 2 dozen pockets.

Nutrition: calories 224, fat 12, fiber 5, carbs 15, protein 5

Croissants

Preparation Time: 10 minutes

Cooking Time: 1 hours

Serving: 8

Ingredients:

A single cup of milk

4 cups of flour that is all-purpose

A third of a cup of sugar that is granulated

2 and a quarter teaspoons of salt that is kosher

4 teaspoons of yeast that is active and dry

A cup and a quarter of butter that is cold and unsalted

An egg wash (this is to have a single large egg, and you beat it with a teaspoon of water)

Directions:

Place your yeast and salt along with the flour and sugar in a bowl and whisk it all together until it has combined well.

Slice your butter into slices an eighth of an inch thick and toss it into the flour mix so that the butter is coated.

Add your milk in and stir it together. A stiff dough will be made.

Wrap your dough and make sure it's tight. You are going to use plastic wrap. Let it chill for 60 minutes.

Get yourself a lightly floured surface and roll your dough into a big and long rectangle.

Fold and make it like a letter. This means you fold it into thirds. Turn it 90 degrees and repeat 4 times.

The dough should be flat and smooth with streaks of butter in it.

Rewrap it again and chill for another 60 minutes. Divide the dough in half and then roll again.

It should be an eighth of an inch thick.

Cut your dough into triangles that are long and skinny.

Notch your wide end of each triangle you made with a half-inch cut.

Roll from the wide end to the end with a point. Tuck the point under the croissant.

Place on a baking sheet that is lined with parchment.

Cover with plastic wrap (loosely) and allow it to proof for 120 minutes.

Preheat your oven to 375 F.

Brush the croissants with your egg wash.

Bake 20 minutes.

They should be a puffy brown golden color, and they should be flaky.

This recipe will give you a dozen croissants.

Nutrition: calories 294, fat 12, fiber 1, carbs 31, protein 5

Junior master chef

Egg Bread

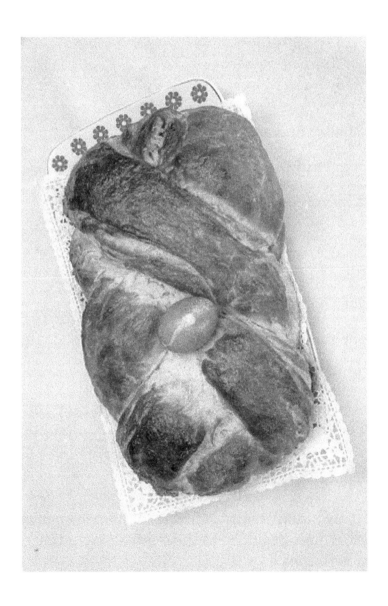

Preparation Time: 10 minutes

Cooking Time: 2 hours

Serving: 7

Ingredients:

½ tsp. of nutmeg powder

3 tsp. of stevia

8 eggs shelled and whisked

1 tsp. of gelatin powder

1 ½ tsp. of active dry yeast

4 tsp. of melted butter

¼ cup of softened cream cheese

1 tsp. very hot water

1 tsp. of cinnamon powder

Directions:

Mix the eggs and the cream cheese that has been softened, unsalted melted butter, and stevia in a mixing container.

In another container, pour the hot water over the gelatin to hydrate it.

Pour the two mixtures into the bread machine pan as per the instructions provided in the manual, including how to pour in the yeast.

Set the machine to basic bread. and when the bread is ready, extract the bread from the pan and place it on a metal mesh surface to cool.

Cut and serve.

Nutrition: calories 178, fat 7, fiber 1, carbs 22, protein 4

Ciabatta Loaf

Preparation Time: 10 minutes

Cooking Time: 2 hours

Serving: 7

Ingredients:

Unsalted melted butter in one teaspoon

Warm water in one cup

3 tsp. of olive oil, preferably extra virgin

2 ½ tsp. of dry yeast

Baking powder in one and a half teaspoons

Husk flour, psyllium in one cup

1 cup of almond flour

Half a tsp. of salt

Directions:

Place the dry yeast on the bread pan.

Get a mixing container and mix the almond flour, husk flour, salt, and baking powder together.

In another mixing bowl, combine the warm water, extra virgin olive oil, and melted butter until thoroughly mixed.

Pour the dry and wet ingredients into the bread machine pan as per the instructions on the bread machine manual, including those of adding in the yeast.

Set the machine at basic bread setting, and when ready, extract the bread and place it on a mesh metal surface to cool.

Cut it and serve.

Nutrition: calories 240, fat 7, fiber 4, carbs 12, protein 12

Pecan and Red Onion Loaf

Preparation Time: 10 minutes

Cooking Time: 2 hours

Serving: 7

Ingredients:

Almond flour in two cups

Coconut flour in one cup

Dry yeast, active in one and a half teaspoons

Red onion cut into small pieces in half a cup

Salt, one and a quarter teaspoons

Unsalted melted butter in a quarter a cup

Warm water in one cup

Pecans that are chopped in half a cup

Walnuts that are chopped in half a cup

Directions:

In a mixing container, mix the almond flour, coconut flour, red onion, salt, pecans, and walnuts that have been chopped.

Follow this by mixing the warm water and melted butter in another mixing bowl.

Pour the mixture into the bread machine pan as per the instructions on the manual, including those on how to properly add in the yeast.

Select the basic bread setting and the crust type, if available, and press start.

When the bread is ready, extract the bread, and place it on a mesh surface to cool.

Slice and serve when completely cool.

Nutrition: calories 129, fat 6, fiber 2 carbs 28, protein 6

Vegetable Bread

Preparation Time: 50 minutes

Cooking Time: 3 hours

Serving: 8

Ingredients

3 ½ cups wheat flour

1 cup water

1 tablespoon salt

1 tablespoon brown sugar

2 tablespoons paprika

Dry herbs (to taste) and vegetables: sweet pepper (green and red), carrots

1 ½ tablespoons oil

2 teaspoons dry yeast

Directions

Add ingredients (water, flour, salt, sugar, oil, yeast) to the bread maker in the manner recommended by the manufacturer of your bread maker.

Turn on the Basic mode.

After the signal, add the paprika, dried vegetables, and herbs.

The final product will be delicious and fluffy bread with a crispy crust that is suitable for every day.

Nutrition: calories 241, fat 4, fiber 3, carbs 46, protein 6

Chapter 10:

Baked dessert and pizza recipes

Beginners

Blondies

Preparation time: 10 minutes

Cooking time: 20 minutes

Servings: 12

Ingredients:

A single cup of melted and unsalted butter

2 and a half cups of flour that is all-purpose

2 large eggs and a single egg yolk

A cup and a quarter of brown sugar that has been tightly packed

Half a cup of sugar

2 teaspoons of vanilla extract

A single cup of walnuts that are chopped

⅔ of a cup of white chocolate chips

Half of a teaspoon of baking powder

2 teaspoons of cornstarch

Directions

Preheat your oven to 350 F.

Line a 13 by 9 pan with parchment paper.

Combine your sugar and melted butter in a bowl.

Add your yolk, eggs, and vanilla extract and then stir until everything has been fully combined.

Set this to the side.

In another bowl, whisk your other ingredients together except the nuts and chocolate chips.

Then fold the nuts and chips in.

Put the batter in the pan.

Put it in the oven and bake for a half-hour.

Let cool.

Nutrition: calories 346, fat 7, fiber 7, carbs 12, protein 4

Intermediate

Snickerdoodles

Preparation time: 10 minutes

Cooking time: 20 minutes

Servings: 12

Ingredients:

2 eggs

Half of a cup of shortening

A half of a cup of softened butter

A cup and a half of white sugar

2 teaspoons of cinnamon that is ground

2 tablespoons of white sugar

2 teaspoons of extract of vanilla

A single teaspoon of baking soda

2 teaspoons of tartar (cream of tartar)

2 ¾ cups of flour that is all-purpose

Directions

Heat up your 400 F.

Cream the butter, sugar, eggs, vanilla, and shortening before blending in tartar, soda and flour.

Shape your dough and put it into balls.

Mix up your sugar (the tablespoons) and cinnamon.

Roll your dough in that mix.

Bake 10 minutes.

Remove right away from the baking sheets.

Nutrition: calories 176, fat 7, fiber 7, carbs 12, protein 10

Apple Pie

Preparation time: 10 minutes

Cooking time: 20 minutes

Servings: 12

Ingredients:

A quarter teaspoon of ground ginger

Half a cup of sugar

Half a cup of brown sugar that is packed

A single teaspoon of cinnamon that is ground

3 tablespoons of flour that is all-purpose

A single tablespoon of lemon juice from a lemon

A single tablespoon of butter

A single, double-crust pie

Half a dozen tart apples that are sliced thinly

A single white large egg

A quarter teaspoon of nutmeg that is ground

Directions

Get a bowl and combine the spices, flour, and sugars.

In another bowl, put in the lemon juice and toss the apples in it.

Add in the sugar mix and toss so they are coated.

Line the pie plate with bottom crust and trim so that it is even with the edge.

Fill it with the apple mix and dot with butter.

Roll the rest of the crust on top to fit the top.

Place it over the filling.

Trim before sealing and fluting the edges.

Cut slits into the crust.

Beat the egg white until it becomes foamy and brush it over that crust.

Place sugar over it.

Cover those edges with foil but do it loosely.

Bake for 25 minutes at a heat of 375.

Take off the foil and bake until the crust is a golden brown color and the filling is nice and bubbly.

This will take an additional 25 minutes.

Let it cool on a wire rack.

Nutrition: calories 176, fat 7, fiber 7, carbs 12, protein 10

Junior master chef

Fruitcake Pie

Preparation time: 10 minutes

Cooking time: 40 minutes

Servings: 8

Ingredients:

1 (9") single-crust pie dough

¼ cup candied pineapple (chopped)

¾ cup red candied cherries (divided)

½ cup packed brown sugar

½ cup dates (chopped)

½ cup light corn syrup

1 cup pecan halves (divided)

6 tbsp butter (softened)

3 large eggs (room temperature and lightly beaten)

¼ tbsp each ground ginger, cloves and nutmeg

Directions:

On a lightly-floured clean work surface, roll the dough out into a ⅛" thick circle. Transfer to a 9" pie plate. Trim the crust so it's ½" over the pie plate's rim, and flute the edges. Put aside.

Chop ½ cup of pecans and put the remaining ½ cup aside. Chop ½ cup of cherries, halve the remaining cherries and put aside.

In a bowl, combine the dates, pineapple, and chopped pecans and cherries and scatter them over the crust.

Next, in a small bowl, cream the butter with the brown sugar until fluffy and light.

Beat in the eggs together with the corn syrup, ginger, cloves and nutmeg. Pour the mixture over the fruit mixture and decorate with the pecan and cherry halves, set aside earlier.

Bake the pie in the oven set at 350 degrees F, until set, for 35-40 minutes.

Then, allow the pie to cool on a wire baking rack.

Serve and enjoy.

Nutrition: calories 576, fat 7, fiber 7, carbs 42, protein 16

Gingerbread-Spiced Pumpkin Pie

Preparation time: 10 minutes

Cooking time: 50 minutes

Servings: 8

Ingredients:

Pastry for 1 single-crust pie

Filling:

2 large eggs (lightly beaten)

1½ cups canned pumpkin

1 cup evaporated milk

⅔ cup sugar

⅓ cup water

¼ cup dark molasses

⅓ tbsp ground cinnamon

½ tbsp ground ginger

½ tbsp salt

¼ tbsp ground cloves

⅓ tbsp ground nutmeg

Whipped cream (to garnish)

Directions:

First, preheat the main oven to 425 degrees F.

On a lightly-floured clean work surface, roll the dough into a ⅛" thick circle. Transfer the pastry to a 9" pie plate. Trim the crust to ½" beyond the plate's rim, and flue the edges. Transfer to the fridge while you prepare the filling.

Next, add the filling ingredients to a bowl (eggs, canned pumpkin, milk, sugar, water, dark molasses, ground cinnamon, ginger, salt, cloves and nutmeg). Whisk to combine and pour into the crust. Bake the pie in the oven on the lowest rack for 15 minutes.

Turn the oven temperature down to 350 degrees F and continue to bake the pie for 30-35 minutes, until springy to the touch. Then, cool the pie on a wire baking rack and serve within 2 hours.

Garnish with whipped cream to serve.

Nutrition: calories 336, fat 30, fiber 7, carbs 12, protein 5

Chapter 11 :

Nutritional values

Remember the Nutritional Facts labels we talked about at the beginning of the book? Those are the labels that tell us what we're eating and how those foods would help us in our efforts to eat healthy and to keep our diets balanced. Those little percentages on the label tell us how much of those things we should be having each day, so our diets are nice and balanced! As mentioned, when we talked about those Nutritional Facts labels, you can get pretty sick if you spend a long time in your life eating too many of the wrong foods and not enough of the right foods. That's why doctors and scientists have come together to make helpful guidelines that we can follow to eat all the right things and to keep the not-so-good things in a healthy balance. When you're trying to put together a meal, you want to make sure that your meals are put together, so the amounts of the foods on your plate look a lot like this one here:

Each day, you want to make sure that you're getting enough protein, healthy fats, natural sugar, and complex carbohydrates that your body can break down and use for energy all day long. A breakfast of eggs, toast, and yogurt is a great way to start your day with protein, carbs, and healthy fats.

A breakfast of chocolate sugary cereal and a donut might leave you bouncing off the walls for a couple of hours and then cranky and sleepy until lunch, so it's best to avoid those kinds of things!

A note to grown-ups

Here are a few more tips to make cooking with your child a stress-free, fun, memorable experience that will set them up for a lifetime love of cooking:

Approach the recipes as an activity. Focus on the process rather than the end result. If your child exclaims, "I made it myself!" or "It tastes great!" at the end, that's all that matters. These results don't have to look perfect.

Plan to cook when you have time. This will result in the most relaxed and fun experience for both of you. Weekends and rainy days are great for this sort of activity.

Allow your child to taste, smell, and touch things along the way. Cooking is an amazingly sensory experience!

Give up some control. When safety isn't a concern, feel free to let your child take the lead.

Start small and build on skills. Give kids tasks they can reasonably accomplish and feel successful about, then expand their repertoire of skills.

Set expectations. Kids are naturally impatient, so when making recipes that might have a long baking or cooking time, let them know what to expect before getting started.

Clean up along the way. This is a good habit for kids to learn, but it will also help prevent you from being left with a pile of dishes at the end of a recipe!

Conclusion

This book is written to motivate your child to enjoy every moment while preparing any recipe and have fun in the kitchen. From cookies and cakes to pizzas and pastries, there are plenty of fun and delicious desserts here for you to explore.

We, as adults, understand the importance of a healthy diet. Those who have learned that at a young age, what is a healthy diet, it is easier to stay healthy into adulthood.

Those who didn't necessarily have the healthiest diets growing up often struggle with their weight and health. At any point in life, people choose to eat healthily and get healthy, but surely from the start you want your children to eat healthy. A child can start helping you cook at a very young age as long as you advise them and hand them things to do that is within their skill level. It is also the best way to get them interested in healthy foods.

In the kitchen, you have to practice in order to get better at it. Ensure that there is no need to get frustrated when things are not going as planned in a recipe because everyone can mess up while cooking. You just got to be patient and ask for help if you need it.

What comes to our mind firstly when we think about baking, are breads, cakes and cookies, in other words, desserts! But what most people don't know is that there are many other baking options that we´ll show you in this book. We could say that baking is the act of cooking something that normally is flour-based, and it is baked in an oven. It's important to know that baking is somehow different than cooking and it could be harder. There is a certain science behind many baking recipes. This is why finding the perfect balance when it comes to the ingredients could be challenging. In this book, there are over 100 recipes for you to practice and improve your baking skills.

The plan of this book is for you to learn important skills in order to be successful in the kitchen, you´ll also find some tips to develop good cooking habits.

Best wishes.

Resources

Green & Black's

http://www.greenandblacks.co.uk/our-range/Bars/Maya-Gold-60?p=2673&c1=1559#first

Scharffen Berger [Semisweet 62% cacao] you might prefer 70%

http://shop.scharffenberger.com/Chocolate-Bars/c/ScharffenBerger@Chocolate@Bars

Taza Chocolate

https://www.tazachocolate.com/collections/discs/products/chipotle

Theo Chocolate

https://www.theochocolate.com/chocolate-bars

Valrhona

https://www.valrhona-chocolate.com/baking-products/baking-chocolates.html

http://www.wilton.com/shop-sprinkles

Cookie sheets

http://www.wilton.com/17x11-jelly-roll-pan/2105-968.html#start=6

Square pans 8 x 8 glass or stainless steel/nonstick

Wilton:

http://www.wilton.com/8-inch-square-pan/2105-956.html#srule=new-arrivals&sz=30&start=90

Wilton Recipe Right Nonstick 12-Cup Regular Muffin Pan

http://www.wilton.com/recipe-right-12-cup-muffin-pan/2105-954.html

Cupcake liners: paper, greaseproof, silicone

Online store:

http://www.bakeitpretty.com/cupcake-liners

Reynolds Wrap Foil Baking Cups 32 Count (Pack of 8) Total 256 Cups

Wilton Silicone 12 Count, Standard Baking Cups, Pastel Round

Wilton Disposable 12-inch bags

http://www.wilton.com/12-inch-disposable-decorating-bags/2104-1273.html#q=12+inch+piping+bags&start=15

Cupcake Piping Tip Set – 4 decorating tips and 8 disposable piping bags.

http://www.wilton.com/cupcake-piping-tip-set/2104-1364.html

CPSIA information can be obtained
at www.ICGtesting.com
Printed in the USA
BVHW040606100321
602119BV00005B/763

9 781914 136429